P9-DGD-129

# THE GIFT THAT ARRIVES BROKEN

# THE GIFT THAT ARRIVES BROKEN

Jacqueline Berger

Autumn House
Press

PITTSBURGH

**Autumn House Press Staff**
Editor-in-Chief and Founder: Michael Simms
Executive Director: Richard St. John
Community Outreach Director: Michael Wurster
Co-Director: Eva-Maria Simms
Fiction Editor: Sharon Dilworth
Coal Hill Editor: Joshua Storey
Assistant Editor: Evan Oare
Editorial Consultant: Ziggy Edwards
Media Consultant: Jan Beatty
Tech Crew Chief: Michael Milberger
Intern: Christina Haaf

This project was supported by the Pennsylvania Council on the Arts, a state agency, through its regional arts funding partnership, Pennsylvania Partners in the Arts (PPA). State government funding comes through an annual appropriation by Pennsylvania's General Assembly. PPA is administered in Allegheny County by Greater Pittsburgh Arts Council.

ISBN: 978-1-932870-36-7
Library of Congress: 2009939551

For my mother and my father

# CONTENTS

## I

## II

**III**

# ONE

## AT THE HOLIDAY CRAFTS FAIR

My friend and I sell compasses
next to a girl selling goddess magnets.
She's so female the air around her
is perfumed—crushed lavender,
curry soup. She's in her twenties
and has a baby who all day travels
from hip to lap. Both of them
blond and every part of their bodies
pumped full, the abundance
of nature bursting into life.
I remember learning to shade in art class,
circles darkened from below
until they were globes.
A useful skill considering the lips
and cheeks, the belly and ass.
Watching the girl as she walks across the room—
her hips in a stretch skirt,
her milk-rich breasts straining the cotton tee—
almost makes me a believer.
And when she pops a breast
out of her shirt to nurse, I can feel
it in my mouth, both the nipple
and the firm swell of flesh around it.
Midday, her friend comes to join her.
They talk of remedies, essential essences,
they praise the Goddess,
passing the child between them.
Then the dad arrives.
He's Venezuelan, tall and so thin his hips
jut out where his stomach dips in.
He's loose as a hinged board, slow as oil.
Now I want to marry both of them,
let the swollen river of their nights
gush over me.
Okay, the woman's views are daft
and the man's English needs work,

and they just moved out of their one-bedroom
to a converted garage. But youth,
that country I never felt at home in,
is bright as sun on water
and shines on them.
Their skin is a place to settle,
a philosophy, a way of life.
He comes back from the food booth carrying pie
with whipped cream. They eat it
together, the spoon dipping
into one mouth then the other.
The baby is happy, gurgling
at the nipple. The woman
is blessed, she tells us during a lull
between customers, and I believe it,
blessed in a way I've never been,
cradled in her body, using it
for every purpose it was intended for.
Thanksgiving's just around the corner,
the feast day's table around which
my own family will gather.
My father being helped to his place
by the caregiver, who settles him in,
ties a napkin around his neck.
He's messy as a toddler now,
suddenly left-handed, his whole
right side refusing to work.
Next to him, my mom, hunched
but tough, my brother who is loud,
the husband I married in my forties.
We will drink wine left over from the wedding,
lift our glasses to each other, here at the table
at the start of one more winter, then
lower our heads to the meal.

## THE FAILURE OF LANGUAGE

First day of class, I ask the students, by way
of introduction, what they believe:
Language is our best tool, or language fails
to express what we know and feel.
We go around the room.
Almost everyone sides with failure.
Is it because they're young,
still find it hard to say what they mean?
Or are they romantics, holding music and art, the body,
anything wordless as the best way in?
I think about the poet helping his wife to die,
calling his heart helpless as crushed birds
and the soles of her feet the voices of children
calling in the lemon grove, because the tool
must sometimes be bent to work.

Sitting next to my friend in her hospital bed,
she tells me she's not going to make it,
doesn't think she wants to,
all year running from the deep she's now drowning in.
I change the flowers in the vase,
rub cream into her hands and feet.
When I lean down to kiss her goodbye,
I whisper I love you, words that maybe
have lost their meaning, being asked to stand
for so many unspoken particulars.

The sky when I walk to the parking lot
this last weekend of summer
is an opal, the heat pinkening above the trees
which dusk turns the color of ash.

Everything we love fails, I didn't tell my students,
if by fails we mean ends or changes,
if by love we mean what sustains us.
Language is what honors the vanishing.

Or is language what slows the leaving?
Or does it only deepen what we know of loss?

My students believe it's important
to get the words right.
Once said, they can never be retrieved.
It takes years to learn to be awkward.
At their age, each word must be carefully chosen
to communicate the yes, but also leave room
for the not really, just kidding, a getaway car
with the engine running.

Inside us, constellations,
bit thread knotted into night's black drape.
There are no right words,
if by right we mean perfect,
if by perfect we mean able to save us.

Four of us pack up our friend's apartment.
Suddenly she can't live unassisted.
I remember this glass, part of a set
I bought her years ago
when she became for a time a scotch drinker.
I bought it for its weight, something
solid to hold, and for the way an inch or two
of amber would look against its etched walls.
I wrap it in newspaper and add it to the box marked Kitchen.

It's my friend herself who is fragile.
When I take her out to eat, each step is work.
The restaurant is loud and bright.
She wants to know if she looks normal.
I make my words soft. Fine,
which might be the most useless word in English,
everything is going to be fine.

## THE MAGIC SHOW

Six of us go on a Saturday night
to a magic show.
The magician stuffs a red silk scarf
into the top of his fisted hand,
pulls out a green one from the other end,
then opens his hand to show
it's empty.
He swallows a deck of cards,
then pulls a black heart
from under his tongue,
circles his neck with diamonds.
A twenty dollar bill that's burned
is later peeled from an orange.
This guy is good,
the sleight of hand, faster
than the eye that tries to follow,
but it's nothing compared
to what I saw the day you died.
I lay on the floor beside you
when the vet gave the shot
and I watched life
vanish into thin air.
No cloth draped then removed
with a flourish, no crate
with a hidden, inner panel.
Death replaced life,
and I have no idea how it's done.

My friends and I sit in the dark
with our drinks, happily baffled.
After the show, we walk out into the night.
The new moon is drawn with invisible ink.
Summer is disappearing into autumn
and we pull our jackets closer.
By morning the mind will want answers.

For a little while amazement is enough.
*Good thing the floor is there*
the magician said when an ace
flipped loose from the deck,
*otherwise this card would fall forever.*

## HOME VISIT

If I start with my father I'd say this,
that he is soft as chalk smudged on thick paper
with the side of the thumb.
Gone into himself, though what that's like
is a mystery, shut in, shut down, deep into the deep
of himself.

Late July. The sun glows in the trees at dusk.
He doesn't want to sit in the yard.
He will, if I coax him. Why does it matter to me?
He wants to sit in his chair with the lever
in the living room, doesn't care if I open the window,
isn't hot. He's been reading the biography of Einstein
for a year, since last July when I bought it
for his birthday. He spends an hour
every morning on the comics, then switches
to relativity. If I am going to place my father
in the harsh light, will I stand beside him?

The trees a lit green against the silk
of sky, a shimmer
as if what lived inside us
could not be contained.
I want my father to sit in the yard.
It's August, or nearly so. Shouldn't he want,
and if not, why not, the slow dance
of summer, its off-the-shoulder nights,
its breath that smells of fruit?

It did not occur to me at sixteen
when I lived here
to ride my bike across the city to the beach,
half an hour and I'd be there.

These weeks I ride there almost
every day, the city practically tropical,

palm trees and hibiscus.
Behind me, the castle of the past.
In front of me, the clean sweep
of sand, water, people I do not know
and will never meet.

She is sixteen but never rides
to the beach, though
in half an hour she could be there.
Never thinks the city can be crossed
so easily, her body a simple extension
of the bike, a few hills, the whole way
on side streets, lovely as the tropics,
swaying palms, hibiscus.
At sixteen, she is matronly.
She stays home, and in the narrow
and crowded, and in the cluttered
and familiar, and in the voiceless
and acute decade of her removal
she eats milk and sugar. She does not eat
hamburgers and fries, does not
frequent places where such food
is served, though other teens do, she knows.
It does not occur to her,
and will not for years to come,
to tell anyone who she is.
She has figured out how she will live,
only worries about how strange
and lonely it will be.

Years later she will ride her bike to the beach,
home to visit, and sometimes
she will stand up on the bike to pedal harder,
as though each next step were a threshold,
one she could not wait to enter.

I was a girl with the body of a woman
from another era, breasts and stomach,
thighs white and thick as dough.
What does this have to do with my father
and the slow way he is vanishing himself
from his life?

Distance is a tool of attachment,
no arrival without departure
and each a heightened occurrence.
After dinner my parents watch Jeopardy,
my mother calling out the answers.
*Who* is Montgomery Clift, Jean Harlow,
the mind like a pocket of loose change.
I'm going on a walk, I tell them from the doorway,
vague wave goodbye. My father looks up,
wants me to stay, says nothing.
Streets without sidewalks, someone's idea
of a village carved into the city
like flowering vines inked into the flesh of the back.
I am trying to get to the center,
though there is no center,
or everywhere is.
My favorite houses are high up,
long stairways, or lowered,
stairs from street level leading down.
A wall of flowers, a curtain,
a chandelier of blossoms dangling
from the canvas ceiling of the sky.

I walk into and am vanished in the purple black,
the color behind the eyelids,
the first dark of night.
I am walking into a dream of walking.
My parents are there, holding the last handful
of their years. They are the stakes in the tent,

the pole that pitches the canvas, peaks its roof.
One day I will walk these streets weeping.

If there were a lake, this would be the hour of bats
swooping to the water, taking an edge
in their mouths and folding it over or lifting it up.
No lake but lawns gone black and wavy.
And then there's the modesty of trees
undressing in the dark. Like matrons,
they let down their hair, unhook
what holds them in, bend at the middle,
lean into each other.
I walk beneath the bridge of their bodies.
I will return to the village years after,
walk the streets weeping,
so alone the trees alone will hear me.

## AT THE EDGE OF THE VINEYARD

When my husband comes to join me
after my days alone
in the room I've made mine,
I free a hook, move the books
off the side of the bed he'll sleep on.
We enter the vineyard at dusk, July heat still in the sky,
walk down its long rows, the grapes
a chalky purple from the yeast that coats them,
the stars, a tangled string of lights.
We hold hands, go farther.
A rabbit in the distance.
Happiness, a quiet guest.

The years I was not human,
my father calls his time at war.
So wine tasting the next day,
pictures of the vintner, a general,
ribbons and medals,
posing beside a plane, are obscene
I tell my husband, quietly
between pours. You don't usually talk
about how proud you are
of your father, my husband says,
after the tasting, in the vintner's garden,
gentle drunk in the sun.

A peeling back of anger, sorrow,
down to what I love
in the men I love.
The pressed oneness we all, don't we,
hope to achieve. Have fun,
the pourer said to the couple leaving.
We're already having fun, one said,
a loose wave, and it was our turn.

I think, my husband said later, looking for wood
to knock, we're going to make it.
Funny verb, make, as though our lives
were something to sculpt or throw,
something with weight and depth.

At dinner, Jews at the next table
embarrass me, their large group talking loudly
about sex. *Whatever's too small
is what I'm just larger than*, the bald guy shouts
and they all crack up.
I can't stop listening,
though my husband tries to bring me back.

We pass on dessert. Stop at the Safeway,
pick up a carton of ice cream,
eat it by our vineyard.

That night I dream of a courtyard
in a poem, or a poem in a courtyard,
and I am calling his name.
A question flowers to another question.
The cave of the blossom is dark.
Low-hanging branches reflected in the water
move like a sequined dress in sunlight
where a woman dances slowly, by herself, in the window.

## THE ROUTINE AFTER FORTY

Because my mother doesn't ask questions—
not the way I would, grilling the oncologist
until she ripped a corner off the examining-table paper
and drew it out—I don't really understand
what it means to have the markers for cancer.
But later in the week, the technician
giving me a mammogram is surprisingly clear
when I ask her, and reassuring. Everyone's body
produces cancer cells all the time,
she tells me. She's blond and ample,
looks like someone who could fix
a leaky sink, then make a pie
to take to a party. But we slough off
the irregular cells, catching early
whatever bad is pitched our way.
Listening to her, I love my body,
its diligence, the work I know nothing about.
Markers in the blood show the body no longer able
to do this. I've shed my paper jacket,
the one handed to me so I would feel less naked
as my breasts lay on the glass plate
like fish on ice. When the jacket slipped,
I let it fall, so now I'm standing here
topless with a little sticker like a pasty
on each nipple, a reference point for the radiologist.
The technician and I have passed the formality
of modesty. Bad things bombard us daily
but for years we are stronger than what will kill us.
You can get dressed now
she tells me, but what I want
is to put my head in her lap,
have her stroke my hair while I tell her
how much I will miss my mother
when she is gone.

The markers of grief,
because my body will accommodate
the vast loneliness of my life without my mother.
My head in the technician's lap,
her fingers lacing my hair,
tell me again about how hard the body tries,
how most of the time it wins.

## WHY I'M HERE

Because my mother was on a date
with a man in the band, and my father,
thinking she was alone, asked her to dance.
And because, years earlier, my father
dug a foxhole but his buddy,
sick with the flu, asked him for it, so he dug
another for himself. In the night
the first hole was shelled.
I'm here because my mother was twenty-seven
and in the '50s that was old to still be single.
And because my father wouldn't work on weapons,
though he was an atomic engineer.
My mother, having gone to Berkeley, liked that.
My father liked that she didn't eat like a bird
when he took her to the best restaurant in L.A.
The rest of the reasons are long gone.
One decides to get dressed, go out, though she'd rather
stay home, but no, melancholy must be battled through,
so the skirt, the cinched belt, the shoes, and a life is changed.
I'm here because Jews were hated
so my grandparents left their villages,
came to America, married one who could cook,
one whose brother had a business,
married longing and disappointment
and secured in this way the future.

It's good to treasure the gift, but good
to see that it wasn't really meant for you.
The feeling that it couldn't have been otherwise
is just a feeling. My family
around the patio table in July.
I've taken over the barbequing
that used to be my father's job, ask him
how many coals, though I know how many.
We've been gathering here for years,
so I believe we will go on forever.

It's right to praise the random,
the tiny god of probability that brought us here,
to praise not meaning, but feeling, the still-warm
sky at dusk, the light that lingers and the night
that when it comes is gentle.

## EULOGY IN ADVANCE OF DEATH

My mom wants to see what I'll write.
She doesn't want to be called a woman of valor,
what all Jewish women are called at their funerals.
I wasn't thinking of valor, so that's not a problem,
but finding the emblematic story,
the one that reveals and sums up, not easy.
Tell the truth, she tells me, don't just say what's nice.

It's Sunday morning, we're on the patio
reading the Times, me the book review,
her the wedding announcements.
She hates how perfect the couples are,
that their parents are always surgeons
or CEOs, still, she reads these first, without fail.
No open casket,
but end the service graveside.
If I'm the last one there,
still standing by the open wound
of earth, my hands covered in dirt,
who will let the caterers into the house?
Maybe I'll give them a key beforehand,
tell them to leave a bucket of water
by the door for the ritual hand washing
so we can rub off the surface cells of grief.

I reheat my mother's coffee and my own,
bring the cups back to the table.
She's moved on to art, an exhibit at the Frick
she'll never see, her traveling days mostly over.
Why not a trivia quiz instead?
My mother's favorite fruit,
favorite flower, favorite scent.
I'll make it the kind of funeral she'd want,
and then I'll be sad all over again, wishing she were there
to enjoy it. We'd go over the details after,

the way we always do, analyzing the small points
of dress and speech.
I like to think I'll stand before the mourners
and say what's true.
Blueberries, lilac, rain.

I should find out what she wants to be buried in,
whether she wants to keep her wedding ring
or if I can have it.
We can talk this way.
Maybe that's what I'll say, half to those gathered
before me, half to the coffin next to me.
Play Edith Piaf, she tells me.
I imagine the sultriness of goodbye,
the heavy velvet of its drape.
I will say that my mother loved me, and loves me still,
the light from the stars not over
though the stars themselves are gone.
Maybe I'll also mention that she didn't take me to college
the first time I left home. No going away party.
No heart to heart to mark the end
of our lives together. I moved on
without ceremony.

Perhaps I'll talk about my bottle collection.
For years after the China exhibit, my mother
bought me snuffs that had once been tied by rope
to the inside of a robed garment.
I'll talk about the mystery
of bottles painted from the inside.
I should mention the lariat of pearls, my favorite necklace,
the glass pin and the swirly black jacket with the flowered lining,
the articles, saved or sent, hidden stairways,
best bookstores, interviews with poets.

I will run my hands over the wood roof
of her casket and feel the last heat
of my mother on my palms.

Is it bad luck to say goodbye in advance of death,
or is it waiting that's always the mistake?
Years later I'll still think of things I want to tell her
and I'll have to stop myself mid call,
the fingers carrying the memory of numbers
though the combination no longer connects.
They'll call air, the air of no longer in service,
the bruise that comes from hitting nothing.

For a week, we'll drape the mirror,
pin a torn ribbon to our clothes.
I'm thinking of pound cake,
schnapps, though my mother
might find that odd. But this is for us.
Grief will lift from our bodies like wings,
a flared jacket of blackbirds,
the lining made of paradise.

## MY MOTHER'S REFRIGERATOR

I scrape mold from a block of cheddar,
peeling the green shavings into the sink.
My mother is smaller than ever
in her turquoise rubber clogs,
pegged pants and sleeveless shirt,
yet she looms like a heat moon
rising over the overpass in August,
legendary as the light I learned to read by.
A grown daughter returns
to be helpful
in a way a thousand sons
could never be,
every surface subjected
to her scouring.
I retrieve a baked potato
hard as a golf ball
that has rolled into the corner
on the lower shelf,
a petrified slice of lemon,
and a dish of something creamy
filmed in gray.
I fill a bag with old food
and haul it to the trash,
ask my mother if it's okay,
taking over what she has never taken on.

Under the thick rind of the moon—
its old-world light
slightly sour, this side
of the expiration date—
the hoarder and her ruthless daughter.

My mother tells me it's okay.
I sweep the crumbs, stack
the papers she won't toss.
Some day they'll be mine
to do with as I wish.
And the food will be mine,
the encrusted, the furred,
apples that soften to their end,
lamb that hardens.
I'll want to keep it all
just to keep the argument alive.

## AT THE POOL

My father is learning to swim,
this time without the use of an arm
and a leg. He still wants to die,
but he is willing to get back in the pool.
Willing, but worried. How will he
change into his suit in the men's locker room
with his female caregiver?
There's a family dressing room
with private stalls, I tell him,
but he doesn't believe it, has never noticed
this room. Nothing is easy.
He needs a new bathing suit
because he made the caregiver throw out his old one
along with his gym bag months ago.
We can buy one on the way.
The lifeguard will attach the special stairs
that lead into the water.
It won't be that hard.
Finally I stop and let my father talk.
I am trapped in my body, he says,
I just don't want to do this anymore.

In the pool he is afraid at first, then floats
on his back in the caregiver's arms.
When she turns him
on his belly, still holding him,
and he tries to turn his face to breathe
but can't, I see the panic,
my father grabbing at the air
and gulping.
Here is the hook.
The body always wants its life,
like an infant finding the knob
of the nipple and pulling
until the spool of milk unwinds.

## CIGARETTES

I'm not a smoker,
but I always imagine myself with a cigarette
when my brother and I visit our parents' graves.
I don't know why I think we will,
my parents never visit their parents' graves,
no family trips to the Jewish cemetery,
but I'm pretty sure I'll want to make the drive
out to the valley on summer evenings with my brother.
We'll have the windows down and music playing,
and once we get there I'll gather up the lilacs
I bought from the only florist in L.A. who had them—
my mother's favorite, what else could I bring—
and we'll make our way to their site.
I'll put the flowers in the holder,
we'll get comfortable on the ground
and I'll open my pack of cigarettes,
tapping one on the back of my hand
in the exaggerated way of nonsmokers
before touching the flame of the match to the tip.
God, it will be wonderful
to draw the smoke all the way into my chest
then let it out slowly.

The lungs want to be filled,
famously after sex, but maybe also
after sorrow. They want to be warmed,
want something more to work with than air.
So I can also imagine myself smoking
by an open window or on a balcony.
There's a typewriter on a table
and next to it, a small brass ashtray.
I'm alone. No longer married.
No longer anyone's daughter.
But the ocean is nearby.

I'm living off some small money,
and this is what I've bought.
It will be peaceful, having a cigarette,
pausing between one time and the next.

In the cemetery, grief will give way to humor,
the way it does, and before we know it
my brother and I will be laughing
about the family we still completely belong to.
By now I'll look natural with my cigarette,
pulling it away to exhale, bringing it back for more.
Then my brother and I will be quiet,
each gone into our solitude.
And here's where the cigarette will be most cherished.
The smoke will drift around me
while I draw my mother and my father back.
When it's time to go, I'll stand up, lightheaded,
but it won't be bad
to be a little dizzy at a time like this.

## THE GIFT THAT ARRIVES BROKEN

My father wishes the stroke had killed him
the way it did his father and his brother.
He doesn't want to go on
being walked to the bathroom by a woman
whose job it is to keep him from falling.
My father who was the same age
for twenty years, the black more gray,
but other than that the body
he stepped back into every morning
was the same body that marched
across Europe, the one that went out
into the rain to get the car
while his family huddled under the awning.
Now I sit close to him, my arm
around his shoulder, something I never
did before, back when distance
was what I needed to keep
his life from spilling into mine.
My brother used anger,
but now his voice sometimes
softens, falls open.
And the night we go out for drinks
after dropping our parents off at home,
I order something sweet and strong
and we talk about death.
We wander out into its moonless night,
stand in its dark field.
We are near enough to see how the end
might come, and willing
to look into the eyes of the animal
that will tear us apart.
I come close to telling my brother
I love him, something I have

never said before.
He likes to be the one
to wheel our dad in the chair
when we go out for dinner.
We are a family in our last years.
I hold my mother's hand.
My brother gets the door.

**TWO**

## WHAT IS THERE

Look at the heart when it is empty
but for an inch of foul water
at the bottom
that a desperate woman will drink.
Look at the fat man
next to the gaunt woman,
one who says *have to*
the other who says *can't*,
each like a dog
straining at the end of a leash.
Look at the leash
you won't let go of.
Look at wanting nothing
because believing nothing.
Touch the seam where your shadow
is sewn to your body
like a dark wing, wet
as the lid of a garbage can
left upturned on the lawn.
Keep looking,
the way you'd watch waves
on a summer afternoon
folding over each other
and flattening against the shore.
Look at desire,
how it thrives in rocky soil
and on narrow footholds
where the teeth of passion
tear the threads
and the buttons of your costume dangle.
Look at scorched earth
where the fire was,
the ground still warm
to the palm that reaches for it.
Look at longing.
Its bright rash flares

like beads along a string.
Look at wallowing.
Look at silk and down and heavy cream.
Look at the need you have sometimes
to forget yourself.
Look until you can look
at anything.
Look at anything
long enough to love it.

## THE SOLOIST

She's sawing her violin,
fraying the music,
then plucking,
then barely touching
bow to strings,
harmonic,
she vibrates.
She's tiny, up on her toes,
then hunched, bent nearly
in half. She's digging in,
her face turned sideways
against the violin, almost
whimpering
like a woman whose lover
gone a thousand days
will be home in an hour.
This must be what the jackers-off
at peep shows wish their dollars bought them,
not the shoddy imitation,
the *sex act*, but the real deal,
sex, grief, love, god
everything it's possible to feel.
If she were a church,
she'd be revivalist,
speaking in tongues,
overcome by the lord.
She's writhing,
letting Prokofiev's
Violin Concerto No. 1
in D major
fuck her raw.
She's ruthless,
letting nothing
stand in her way.
She's devoured
and devouring.

And we, symphony-goers
in our black
or jewel-toned
evening wear,
sit slack-jawed,
splayed in our seats,
or erect, hands clasped.
We know what we are seeing,
not one of us
doesn't recognize
ourselves,
what we would look like
if we were not too ashamed
to let it out.

## DEVIANT

Three hundred students study bondage
and bestiality, the most popular course
on campus. And the teacher, eighty-two,
in the feature article I'm reading over breakfast,
tells of his own predilections,
prowling Polk St. for rent boys.
The hound of the body
still wants the hunt.
Did the man need to be coaxed to tell,
or did his story pour out of him?
A survey course in sex takes the charge out,
nothing's normal, or everything is.
And who slipped this past the editor,
the news of love and what small
corners it crouches in?

Unapologetic, the man says the old dog
wants to be petted
more than once in a while,
perfunctorily, in passing.
He hasn't cheated gravity or time,
his flesh drapes, his hands are speckled.
Nor has he cheated loneliness
or boredom, but he's not done
living his human life in his human body.

The interviewer could have asked
a hundred different questions
and the man might have told
of washing his mother's bony back
in the weeks before her death,
or of similar acts for friends
who died of AIDS.
Or of the bad old days
when gay was a diagnosis
and of the work of others

to change the nomenclature
and of his own work,
on the sidelines, true,
but in his way trying
to advance another view.
And of decades of students
pouring their hearts out
in essay after essay,
shame and loathing,
and then, god help him,
having to grade those papers
because scholarship had to be maintained
even or especially if the subject was sex.
Could have, no doubt, told
any of this, but wasn't asked
and didn't steer the conversation
away from the truth of his own body.

## AT THE TABLE

Those who practice moderation,
their faces mild and benign,
their plates cleared away
with half their dinner remaining,
don't believe every meal is their last,
but even if this one is,
they're fine leaving some of it untouched.
Then there are those of us who order the bottle
because the best wines
aren't offered by the glass.
We share dessert, but share two of them
because we love both chocolate and plums.
Our off switch doesn't work, Lisa says,
and the next day's punishment of pleasure
is just part of the bargain.
Her dog tosses a stuffed snake across the room
in the gleeful dance dogs do to celebrate a visitor.
He's a big dog, mastiff and pit bull,
scary looking with gold eyes
which makes me want to trust him
the way I'd want to give a thug a second chance.

Joy may be ephemeral
as the full moon swaying on an alpine lake,
but we are like the villagers
in the fairy tale I read as a child
who thought they could scoop
a chunk into their bowls and eat it.
The author intended his young reader
to understand the foolishness of this,
but I loved the villagers,
up all night with their slotted spoons
digging into the milky water.

Maybe they pulled buns from wicker baskets
and shared them with their neighbors,
the floury moon, the custardy moon
one way or another filling their mouths.

The body is the source of joy
but also the servant.
We feel no compunction
keeping it up all night
then calling in the morning for a favor.
And desire is a dog
that's bred to kill,
but we let him in the house
and love him.

## CELEBRITY COOKING

I've set the timer, am doing sit ups
on the exercise ball
and watching the food channel
where the actress is making a salad.
There's green dressing in the blender.
She doesn't eat carbs, no bread or fruit,
they cause cravings, she tells the host,
an ample woman who nods in agreement.
Just vegetables and meat.
The camera is indifferent,
capturing the actress and the host
but also the actress's sullen and beautiful
teenage daughter. Ignored by the adults,
she's a prop, the helper, and at the moment
is digging a spoon into the blender,
again and again, and shoveling the dressing
into her mouth. She must have gotten some
on her hand because now she's sucking
her knuckles, such vigor, her whole fist
seems to be making its way in.
Whether she's oblivious to the camera
or knows exactly what she's doing
is hard to say. If she crammed her hand
down her pants, it wouldn't surprise me.
I call my husband into the room to watch.
Mother and daughter are playing chicken.
The girl, bleak and hard, steps off the curb,
crossing against the light.
The actress, sun-bleached,
doesn't slow, but swerves
at the last minute to miss her.
My husband and I are rapt.
We know something about swallowing rage,
surviving the family.
It's like looking down the wrong end of a telescope,
small and far away, the girl
I'd like to take in my arms but who never
in a million years would let me.

## CIRCUS SCHOOL

*Orders*

Make the body
climb a rope, and it finds a way.
The body's mind
concerned with how,
not why.

*Progress*

Week one, I can't get off the ground.
By the third week, I'm halfway
to the ceiling.
In therapy, five years
talking about fear.

*Relationship*

The mind is a bully,
telling the dog
of the body what to do.
But the mind is also afraid
of the dog, stupid animal
running the show.

*Deeper*

My teacher lies on me
to deepen my stretch.
The body is meant to hurt,
the thought the mind settles on
as I breathe, leg spread wide,
chest pressed to the floor,
the weight of the teacher pushing me down.

*Later I Amend It*

The body wants to choose its pain,
wants its pain to have meaning,
the pain of getting stronger,
the pain of healing,
and the next day's pain
a reminder—I did well, worked hard,
nothing's broken.

*Marriage*

The mind and the body
have good years
when each
values what the other offers,
and bad years,
nothing but blame between them.

*Everything Shows*

The body can't keep a secret.
It parades in the streets
what the mind would prefer
to keep private: Not only
what, but how much
and how often.

*First Weeks*

After class, I'm ravenous.
Can't make it home.
Have to find somewhere
to eat. Turns out
hunger is easy.
Not like loneliness.
Not like longing.

## The Blind Class

They feel their way up the ladder,
grab the trapeze that's put in their hands,
hold on, swing out,
a long arc before letting themselves
fall into the net.
It's not rude to stare.

## Rite of Passage

The day I make it to the top
everyone cheers.
I let myself down from the ceiling slowly,
legs gripping the rope.
On my right thigh, a welt.
Everyone in this room's
had one of those, my teacher says.

## Credit

The mind takes credit
but offers the bicep
for a friend to feel.

## HIGH

The baby rubs her hands in wide circles
on the schoolyard bench
until her palms are dark with dirt.
Running is good. Climbing is good,
but so is squatting and staring,
touching a sun-warm surface
until the hands know something new by feel.
This is how the brain is made.

Stoned feels like the senses
have come alive, but they haven't,
says the scientist, talking to the parents of preteens.
The taste of pancakes, of syrup, butter—
miraculous. Leaves blowing
on the trees, do they always
make that sound? Nothing is still,
everything moving, even stones,
the air around them.
It's not the senses newly alert, he warns,
but memory temporarily nulled
so we don't recall the thousand times before
we've eaten breakfast or walked outside
and can't do the simple matching,
pulling the pancake card from the vault of the mind.
The high is what it's like, floating past memory,
encountering without association.
Tell the kids to wait until they're eighteen
and the brain has finished formulating—
mechanics, not morality, the basis of his talk.

But at forty-eight, I don't want heightened,
I want dulled. Overstimulated all week,
when my husband comes home, Friday night,
with the bag from the store that sells the wine we like,
I'm happier than I should be.

He puts it in the freezer so it'll be ready faster.
The first glass does the work of separating,
as one might slip fingers under the skin of a chicken
to loosen it from the bone, making  a pocket
for the herb paste to be pressed against the flesh.
I am loosened from my datebook,
each day's list of obligations.
The good loss. A friend says it's freeing, too,
when your parents die.
Exhilarating to be an orphan,
no one to answer to. I've wondered
about this. When the loneliness lifts,
if it lifts, will I like the drift,
no longer corseted by the need to please?

Stoned kids, we stood on the overpass at midnight,
stared down at the freeway's river of streaking light.
Walking home, the feel of that whoosh.
We were going eighty, the thrum and jolt of traffic
racing through our bodies.
It doesn't hurt, not like a broken arm.
Brain cells give up without a fight,
a gentle snuffing and they're gone.

Nearing fifty, is it the aftermath of drugs
or the slow recession of estrogen
that makes me so forgetful?
How much of my life, day to day,
do I never transfer to the long-term column,
letting the details dissolve like crystals in water?
Other bits I'll remember forever,
the way the baby clutches pebbles
the whole way home so her palm
when finally pried open
is pocked.

The first time I dropped acid
my friend and I tore up money
and threw it into the sea.
Why do I remember that?
The damage is done, but so, I would have said
at sixteen, is the enlightenment.

## HOLIDAY WEEKEND

A woman buys a dress for the feel
of silk spilling over skin,
then hates the skin.
Maybe it's possible
in some distant world to separate,
make pure, but in this world
we sit in the shade of a grafted tree.
Joy leads but derision follows.
Desire is bound to fear.
Contentment leans its soft flesh
against the spine of dread.
Denial and panic, there's a popular
conundrum.
Grief and boredom,
one hand strokes the head
of the sensitive lover while he weeps,
the other quietly reaches for a book.
Lust and rage, of course.
A fight turned inside out
reveals its satin lining,
its lace panties
with their Saturday-night swagger.
Regret and anything
because who, given a second chance,
couldn't write a better ending?
So the miracle of three perfect days
in spring, on a balcony,
in the new love's arms
are kept like jewels in a velvet box.
Days of doing nothing
but swinging lightly in the hammock
of afternoon, its cradling hours. Nothing
more alarming
than the lover needing his lap
to get a glass of water,
bring it back to share.

A long weekend
is the limit
of unadulterated joy.
The hooded heart returns.
When the flame
from the candle catches
the feather throw,
a corner goes up in smoke.

## HOW WE MAKE IT WORK

I knew a woman once who kept her dog in the garage.
He was a big dog, a golden retriever, too big,
she said, to take on walks. He pulled.
She couldn't control him. Twice a day
she brought him food, kept his water bowl filled.
When he got into the house for a second,
he was hysterical, desperate, jumping on her,
running in circles, his tail sweeping
the delicate arrangement of flowers,
spilling the water. The woman would wrestle
him back into the garage as quickly as possible
the way one tries to stuff a jack-in-the-box
back down after the spring pops the lid.
Why did she want a dog in the first place?
He came with papers. She must have thought
the luxury of gold would add its luster
to her landscape. Instead she had an unruly
animal and a door kept locked against him.
Each day her dog must have hoped
she would kneel down, throw her arms
around him and bury her face in his fur.
Why didn't she get rid of him,
give him to a family with kids who would love
a pet to roughhouse with in the yard?
But perhaps she too loved the dog
the way anorexics love food,
all day yearning for what
they will not let themselves go near.
She needed the dog. Someone
had to tell the truth
about loneliness.
Her husband worked past dinner,
spent his weekends on the couch drinking whiskey
and listening to classical music through headphones.
Let the dog come in the house,

for Christ's sake, I wanted to yell.
He'll calm down once he knows he gets to stay.
Years later I saw how I lived,
how short I kept my leash, how large
the boulder I tied it to.
I pretended to hear nothing,
though in moments of stillness
the whimpering
from behind the locked door
could not be denied.

## THE CONDUCTOR

There's no mention, of course, in the program
that the conductor has Parkinson's.
He enters the stage, stands for a moment
facing the audience,
his hands by his sides, tapping air.
Then he holds them together, an act of gratitude
—we are gathered, we can do this—
and of firmness, each hand forcing
the other to be still.
His expression, darkly bemused,
the good news/bad news:
I've lived long enough to lose so much.
Or maybe he's staving off our sympathy,
don't clap because of this.
Then he turns his back to us, begins his work.
Mendelssohn's Scottish Symphony.
No baton, and from behind
his body is jerky as a boy's,
jumpy with excitement.
His hands shake when they scoop
the sections of the orchestra,
as though pulling a weighted net
from the sea. Still, I wonder if this work
is easier than taking on the ordinary
objects of a day—
buttons, keys, and pens.
I am an old man
he must think when he looks
in the mirror,
briefly naked before trading
the bathrobe for the tie and tails.
And when he turns to us again
after the last movement, he looks both
old and young, his face washed

of the expression in the program photograph,
clearly taken years before,
one eyebrow slightly raised,
his smile more satisfied than happy.
Now he shows us his innocence,
if innocence is what the face
unconstructed can be called.
What else can he do,
while his fingers tap their useless code,
while the audience, in rows, rises from their seats,
still clapping, what can he do
but show us who he is,
a man standing too close to the edge,
edge no one can call him back from.

## IF ALL POEMS ARE ELEGIES

From the story the thirty-something guy
at the hotel-room party is telling me,
both of us lounging on the bed,
his lips lined in red from jug wine,
his mother's death at sixty took him apart.
He's a lawyer who hates his job.
It's his wife in the other room
who's the writer. Hates his job
but, as they say, is ready to call it a life.
It wasn't how I imagined it would be,
he tells me. She was so angry,
puking in the sink the time she came to visit,
yelling at us to stop watching, though how
can you take care and not look?
He's in therapy now, of course.
I like his earnestness, his apologizing:
I shouldn't be telling you all this.
We're both Jews. Does that matter?
New York, L.A., Florida,
triangle of migration so easy to follow.
Next week when I drive down the state
to visit my own family, I'll thank my mother
for living long enough to see me
into the middle of my life.
Once I told her I'd miss her when she was gone,
and she said she'd miss me too.
It's like what the young man tells me,
the living lose one person, but the dying
lose everyone at once.
All elegies are love poems,
and who loves more than the one
standing alone at the edge of the sea,
calling and calling?
I will not kiss the man's wine-traced lips,

but I love the way he presses
his story into mine. After death,
the beloved is air, early snow
and the late sun that comes to melt it.
But love itself remains
with its great impersonal intimacies,
two hours on a bed
or the rest of your living days.

## OTHER PEOPLE'S LIVES

The woman reading her poems
is ahead of me
by maybe fifteen years.
Her mother has already died.
What do I learn by listening?
At nineteen I met my best friend
who at twenty-nine was leaving
what I was entering.
I made her tell me how she lived
that decade of sex and power,
the body at its height,
the mind finally free to spend big,
buy the room a round and bed the bartender.
My friend when I met her
was saying goodbye
to what she knew of lavish,
a summer spent on the canals in Venice,
an affair with a boy who wouldn't speak.
Did he really wear a leather lace-up vest,
or am I embellishing?
Romantic, not disturbing,
their silent afternoons,
getting stoned and eating oranges.
I moved a lot.
That's my youthful claim to fame.
That girl dancing at the concert,
shirt rolled under her breasts,
throwing her head back
in what looks like joy,
that was not me.

The woman reading her poems
says she is grateful
for the eight years of dementia,

each a little darker than the one before,
that led to her mother's death.
Listening to other people
tells us only that we are not alone.
We all go through.
Maybe I will be grateful too
and changed utterly.
What a word, *utterly*.
My mother and I will find
our own way,
or maybe we won't find
anything but have the end
thrown down so hard on us
it will take all of our strength
to lift it.

## THE WEIGHT OF BLOOD

Those years we were both on the cusp,
mine about to start, hers winding down.
I'd be brushing my teeth and she'd be peeing
and when she had her period
the smell of my mother's blood,
mineral and yeast, rose from the belted napkin.
Did she know I could smell it
as easily as I now smell myself every month,
the swift, nostalgic odor when I pull down my pants?
I like the smell, a little sexy, a little grimy,
but back then I could only say it was there.
We never spoke of it, of course,
and it's hard to imagine
I knew my mother when she was my age now.
These days I do all the driving when I visit her—
she gives me the keys, I tower over her,
but she still tells me where to turn.
I park as close as I can, then slow down
to walk at her pace. Her body is curved
as though caving. The cane is new.
The end of the block could be the other side
of the world, but I am happy
to make time hobble, no hurry
to get where it's going.

I never used to keep track
but every month now I record
the number of days between them.
The fact of blood on toilet paper
tells me I'm still on this side.
It's good our bodies don't ask permission
to loosen their grip, let drift off
what needs to go.
The chance to have children
is down to a trickle,

before long the blood itself will stop,
and at some point being a child,
having a mother,
will be over as well.
Yes, it's good our permission
isn't needed.
I'm fine being the grown daughter,
having an aging mother.
After that, what dark waits,
I would put off forever.

## DYING ALONE

A woman you knew
was found two days later,
no one to hear her final Oh
and come running.
Her friend couldn't understand
why she'd missed their lunch,
didn't return calls.
They found her on the floor,
a book or broken cup
near her hand that even in death
reached out to break the fall.
But more than dying alone,
you are afraid of living alone.
The woman never married,
had no children.
She was fifty-seven,
had been unemployed
for over a year, was fat,
and sometimes, truth be told,
she smelled a little like broth.

What you learned at the memorial:
she played Chopin,
was Episcopalian,
got her degree from Stanford,
lost her mother four months earlier.
Forty people came to mourn
her passing. You wondered
how many would come for you.
Your husband is only out of town,
will be home the day after tomorrow.
But the woman's death
has dragged your loneliness forth.
Loneliness you still feel

you've narrowly escaped,
that your fate too was solitude,
the comfort of cherries thickened with cornstarch
under a lattice of crust.
Easy to imagine the bolstering
pep talk in the mirror
the woman needed
to get herself out of the house,
and easy to imagine the pleasure
of returning to cat and nightgown.
Is it too late to say you liked this woman?
She soldiered through,
did not lose her kindness, her wit.
This business of fear
is yours. What she was afraid of,
you'll never know.

# THREE

## GIN

I like a green olive
stuffed with a pimento
after it has been submerged
for some time in a martini.
I like to go downtown with my husband,
sit in a booth at the Grand
and let the drink rub the edge
off the inane fight we had
about the furniture salesman
and whether he treated us fairly,
my view, or whether he tried
to put one over on us,
my husband's view.
In some moods we'll fight about anything
just to make the other
carry the weight of anger
we lug all day through our lives.
But that moment
when we climb into bed
on a winter's night,
letting our bodies lie down,
letting the day be over,
is not unlike the way gin
loosens the rope, lets float
the raft into its stillest waters.
Happy hour, when the landscape
loses its daylight meaning
as it slips into the silk of dusk
before night pours down its jazzy notes
in a cathedral of crushed velvet.
We are sitting side by side in the booth,
watching the flurry of holiday shoppers
come in from the cold.
By now the salesman is a jerk,
or he's a helluva guy,

either way is fine.
We are talking about anything,
having drifted out into the calm
plainness of intimacy. Nothing
profound, just a place to rest
at the end of the day,
the cord between us swinging gently
after the bells have stopped their ringing.

## GOOD

It's good to have a great love of your life
but marry someone else.
Good to keep this great love
in the weedy outfield of the mind
to alternately worship and despise.
It's good to have a week when you think you're dying,
a spot found on your spine or lung.
Good to get your house in order,
unroll the scroll of your life,
finger it fondly and with sorrow.
Even better to learn it's a false alarm,
the spot nothing at all.
It's good to hear this story from your parents' neighbor
one evening in July. He's not that much older
than you are, though he used to be,
when you were a kid and he already a father.
You're in the car, on your way somewhere,
and he's out with his dog, escaping the heat
of the house. He leans against your open window
and at some point you cut the engine
because you know what's best is often told in passing.

It's good to realize you married the right man after all,
to want your life as it is,
though you can imagine other versions
you might like better.
Good to return for the summer
to your hometown,
to the neighborhood that will be there long after
anyone you know still lives in it,
neighborhood whose jacarandas and melaleucas,
whose post-war bungalows and ranches
in their low-slung, humdrum elegance
will always take you back
though you fled at eighteen
as though the city were on fire
or you were.

What's good is a courtyard painted
the color of fruit and strung with lanterns
where you drink wine with your best and oldest friend.
And good is seeing the sky at dusk as painted velvet,
the outline of downtown quickly sketched in white
or chalky blue. It is good sometimes
to have feelings but no words,
to have, instead, pictures—
swimming pools seen from the sky
as the plane is landing, or the ocean coming into view
after miles of hills when the highway suddenly
leans against the coast.
Good to have more than one way to approach.
It's good you married not the one you wanted to love
but the one you actually could love.
Good your parents still live in the house you grew up in,
and good to have a city you long for
but don't live in, afraid to break the spell,
like anything destroyed when held too close.
Good to imagine coming home
though nearly thirty years go by
and you are still imagining.

## TEACHING MY HUSBAND TO SWIM

Usually I'm the one who knows nothing,
frozen at the computer while my husband
tries to talk me through.
But this morning at the inn where we've come
to celebrate our second anniversary,
he tells me how many people in the past
have tried and failed to teach him how to swim.
I throw my suit on and grab our towels.
This is something I know I can do.
We've already been in the pool— a late afternoon
dip when we got here, me doing laps
and my husband dog paddling beside me,
his head above water, or holding his breath
the length of the pool before coming up for air.
Now I stand by the side, pulling my elbows back
and turning my head to demonstrate the crawl.
The fog has burned off the valley
and the pool shines, set off by the vineyards
whose grapes in another month
will be ready for harvest.
My husband in the pool tries to follow what I'm showing
but yanks his head to the surface, coughing water.
I get in with him and we discuss the mechanics
of breathing. He doesn't know about exhaling
through the nose under water, never learned
the significance of making bubbles.
It's a revelation. I send him
back and forth across the pool and it works.
He's swimming. Each time his face comes up
as his arm draws back,
the O of his mouth looks like wonder
or terror. We move on to the breast stroke,
and his head, like a needle stitching cloth,
gathers the water in thick folds.
I stand off to the side coaching,
triumphant but careful to let the victory be his.

An ironic high five when we get out of the water
is all he wants to signify the occasion.
In the delicate economy of marriage
giving costs less than receiving,
the thin wire of power
threaded through the soft body of need.
We're ready for a hot bath
and both fit in the large tub in our room
where we lather our bodies and hair,
passing the soap between us.

## THE SUBJECT OF ENDINGS

I'm pulled from sleep by boys
barely old enough to have a license
joy riding over the hump of our hill.
I go to the window to watch.
The car is airborne before landing hard
on the down slope. The buddies
are standing on the curb, cheering
for gravity and speed, their thin arms
folded against the February night.
They're drinking beer, shivering and happy.

As much as we say we don't, we do,
we love our lives,
the miserable years of our youth,
how odd we were as children,
what our bodies do as we age.
At the base of the hill the boys screech
the car into circles, leave skid marks.
This is their language.
Only here, or in sex, do they drift close.
I leave the window, get back into bed.
My husband is turned away from me in sleep.
I curl against his warmth, then roll
onto my back to be lowered
more easily into the ditch of dreams.

The boys know nothing
of what's to come.
They've left their beds,
maybe even a girl lying beside them,
to stand in the fog with their friends
and do this thing that tells them
they are living.
They will be blindsided by their lives.
I'm a good thirty years ahead of them
and better at saying I saw it coming.

I know enough to mistrust.
New in our marriage,
my husband and I can't say
it will hold.
If we were writing our lives,
either ending might make sense.

No one got hurt.
At the end of the night, the car
was still drivable, the boys still
believed in the sturdiness of matter,
that danger is largely exaggerated.
A good ending clicks shut,
the last word both obvious
and unexpected.
But here is a drifting off,
the boys headed home or somewhere else,
sleep took me back,
the weeks to come, hard
and then better, details
like shards of metal on a magnet.
Each boy, if he remembers this night,
will make it stand for something.
And I too, at the window, watching,
take their night and use it.

## FALSE SPRING

In February, three days
of warm blue. I go sockless,
roll down the windows.
At the stoplight, a man so casually good looking
it hurts to watch
walks with a baby on his shoulders,
the two of them framed in cherry blossoms,
the glorious and early bloom like an open fan
of pink and white.

The light turns, but all day I see them
approaching the crosswalk,
about to step off the curb.
The window when I could have had
a young husband, a baby,
never opened. Up ahead,
my parents' deaths.
My father's will fill me with questions,
but my mother's
will hollow me out.

How quickly it passes.
Outside my mother's bedroom window
as a child, lilacs. There was a man
she loved before my father,
a box of letters in the garage.
A photograph from a trip to Mexico.
There was Berkeley
and Ontario. A long necklace
of blue beads, years she made granola
every Saturday morning from scratch.
There is the mystery of my father's body
as a soldier, the photograph of him
holding a gun. After the war,
the GI Bill, a rented room,

security clearance and the mustache
he grew in the '70s, the mistake of loud plaid,
the jacket he wore once and left
hanging at the back of the closet.

I want to stop traffic, let the man
with the baby on his shoulders
cross so slowly they make time go backwards.
I find a place to park, wander into a store called Nest.
Sorrow gives beauty its power to move us.
This thought nearly compels me
to purchase a fifty-dollar soap dish from Paris,
a necklace for three hundred,
its pale blue-green stone crocheted
in its setting with black thread
because the body must be honored and adorned
for the short time it is ours.
Only the bones are immortal.

By now the man and the baby have reached home.
He fumbles with the key, but his wife
hears him and comes to the door.
Amused as she reaches for the baby
who wears a cherry blossom in her hair
from the walk under the ceiling of flowers.

## SOMETIMES

Do people still go for drives?
My father every Saturday took his mother,
deep in her dementia, to the ocean.
She had stopped bathing.
Her wig was matted, and once
I saw by accident between her legs,
her skirt stretched open,
that she wasn't wearing underwear.
I think that's what I saw, dark clearing
where the trees have parted but the ground
is covered in needles.
Years later my mother told me
how those drives drained my father,
how neither his brother nor sister,
eight and ten years older,
took their turn. My father
was the unexpected
favorite. And so the ocean
before them every Saturday.
What did they talk about
sitting in the car,
because I can't imagine they got out,
nature best from behind glass,
while the ocean modeled how to do
and undo, do and undo?

Now it is my father whose memory is scattershot,
asking again what day it is,
where we are going for dinner,
but then talking to David as he always has
about business or teaching, politics, real estate.
As an earthquake or a fire sometimes takes out
three houses in a row but leaves the fourth untouched,
so too a stroke to the grid of the brain.

Sometimes we are bored and sometimes
we are mesmerized, the over and over
of the ocean, the perseveration of the sun,
endless wheel of the seasons.
I wonder if my father on occasion
after my grandmother died
still drove to the ocean.
Doubtful. As though she,
lost from so much of her life,
needed the reassurance of water,
but he in his grief or regret
or in his emptiness,
could go back to his life,
iron lid on the boiling pot.
To sit alone in the car, the ocean
before him, this I can't imagine.
The medicine of the sea
was something that could wait
until he too, close to his death,
needed to be soothed
by the folding sheets of waves.

## WATCHING THEM SLEEP

First I listen outside the door.
My mother makes a tea kettle sound
since surgery, my father is silent,
the legendary snores mysteriously gone.
Then I crack the door, peer into the dark,
watch the breath lift and lower their bodies,
see my father's good leg twitch under the covers.
I am forty-five next week.
The chance for children as good as over.
One percent the gynecologist said.
The instinct that was supposed to make
me want to change my life, do anything
for a baby, briefly flared and died.
I only wanted something small
to hold, something powdery and soft.
But for the work of caretaking,
I have this, bending to tie my father's shoes,
helping him up when he falls.
I'm not carrying anyone into the world
but out of it. Watching my parents sleep
before returning to my own room
in my in-laws' house in the mountains
where we have gathered for Thanksgiving,
I say into the dark, let this last.
Let night pass through our hands
like a silk cord. In the morning,
let us open our umbrellas, walk carefully
in the rain that higher up the mountain turns to snow.
Let us eat and let us complain
about being too full to ever eat again.
Let us walk it off.
Let us praise November's beauty
which is lovelier than June's
for being mixed with sadness.
Let us love the short days
given over to long nights.

Let us love what is frayed,
what cannot be fixed.
Let our lives that have no purpose
but to be lived
be praised.

## THE MOON NEARS DAWN

Gears groan as the moon is hoisted
nightly into the sky on its chain.
Mornings, the moon is dragged back down
and curls like a small animal
in a wooden bucket, its white fur
filling the circle,
its breathing steady and slow.

We are separated,
the bedtime self altered
imperceptibly from the breakfast self.
Years of this and we are unrecognizable.
Now the daughter on one side
and the son on the other
are in their grown bodies,
they are not swinging their legs under the table,
they know they will continue on alone.

Days are only meadows to the sleeping moon
who dreams of chasing rabbits,
a hunter in hound's flesh.

Can we hold all of our selves at once,
new and full, *not yet*,
and *once when*?

If we stand on the porch with our glass,
we can toast the moon: moon
like a kite in the trees,
moon in the center of the glass eye
the architect built into the domed cathedral
so God could pour his light
down the throats of the faithful,
funnel the light through the hole in the sky,

sift it like flour onto the eyelashes of his flock.
Standing in the courtyard, under the falling snow,
they blink away God's will and *goodnight brother,*
*goodnight sister* to the family of followers.

Longing is a question
rising like the new moon
over a dark field.
Let the family eat in peace,
the mother in her body, the father
in his body, the grown children
close enough to see how soon it will be over.

Winter moon rocks all night in its chair.
It's not that we want what we long for
but that longing is a kind of mourning,
a kind of prayer
to what is leaving or is gone.

## IF WE COULD CHOOSE

It's an old question and maybe a bad one,
whether it is better to die fast,
leaping into the snow-fed lake,
or slow, standing in the shallow end
until the body adjusts to the cold.
A heart attack takes out a man
on his vacation. He goes to bed early,
a little tired. His wife stays
in the lodge before the fire,
yakking to strangers. She's in her element,
and he is happy to leave her to it.

Some say a swift end is a blessing—
he didn't even see it coming.
But death continues taking,
the wife forever rewinding the last day,
rewriting the final scene.

Speed is a trick.
I would rather give away, bit by bit,
everything I own
until, when death comes,
almost nothing is left to take.
I think I could stand
being bedridden for a year,
in the end needing help
with everything.
I'd like the chance to say good riddance
to the body, its vanity, its shame.
Let me float those last months
like a dinghy in the mist.
Let my mind part like reeds
to let the wooden boat through.
If I am in pain, give me
a generous morphine drip.

If I am alone, let me have
the memory of my parents,
my husband, fragments of lovers,
anyone I want
to comfort me.
I want to hand back the keys.
I want to believe in the dignity
of loss, the last great insight,
if there is one, slipping from me
unspoken like a poem
in a dream that is gone
by morning. It was, of course,
a great poem, maybe my best.
In the end, let there be nothing left behind
but a ring such as milk leaves
after it's been scalded in a pan and poured.

## NOTE

"The Failure of Language":
The poet is Jack Gilbert, and the images I refer to are from his
poem "Finding Something."

*The arches of her feet are like voices*
*of children calling in the grove of lemon trees,*
*where my heart is as helpless as crushed birds.*

## ACKNOWLEDGMENTS

Thank you to the following journals where poems from this
collection have previously appeared:

*Atlanta Review*: "Watching Them Sleep"
*Georgia State Review*: "At the Pool"
*North American Review*: "The Routine After Forty"
*Passaic*: "The Gift That Arrives Broken"
*River Styx* and *Poetry Daily*: "My Mother's Refrigerator"
*Smartish Pace*: "Cigarettes"
*Southern Poetry Review*: "What Is There"
*The Iowa Review*: "Gin," "The Weight of Blood," "At the
   Holiday Crafts Fair"


Heartfelt thanks to the many friends who read these poems
along the way and offered their invaluable comments: Melody
Lacina, Laura Horn, Sharon Fain, Ella Eytan, Sandra Nichols,
Nancy Cherry; to the fine baristas at the Dolores Park Café who,
for the cost of a coffee, let me make my office there; to my fam-
ily, source of heat and light. And thank you to my husband, Jeff,
for his steadiness and brilliance, generosity and faith.

## THE AUTUMN HOUSE POETRY SERIES

*The Leaving, New and Selected Poems* by Sue Ellen Thompson
*Dirt* by Jo McDougall
*Fire in the Orchard* by Gary Margolis
▲ *Just Once, New and Previous Poems* by Samuel Hazo
*The White Calf Kicks* by Deborah Slicer • 2003, selected by
  Naomi Shihab Nye
*The Divine Salt* by Peter Blair
▲ *The Dark Takes Aim* by Julie Suk
*Satisfied with Havoc* by Jo McDougall
*Half Lives* by Richard Jackson
▲ *Not God After All* by Gerald Stern (with drawings by
  Sheba Sharrow)
*Dear Good Naked Morning* by Ruth L. Schwartz • 2004,
  selected by Alicia Ostriker
▲ *A Flight to Elsewhere* by Samuel Hazo
*Collected Poems* by Patricia Dobler
*The Autumn House Anthology of Contemporary American
  Poetry* edited by Sue Ellen Thompson
*Déjà Vu Diner* by Leonard Gontarek
*lucky wreck* by Ada Limón • 2005, selected by Jean Valentine
*The Golden Hour* by Sue Ellen Thompson
*Woman in the Painting* by Andrea Hollander Budy
*Joyful Noise: An Anthology of American Spiritual Poetry*
  edited by Robert Strong
*No Sweeter Fat* by Nancy Pagh • 2006, selected by Tim Seibles

*Unreconstructed: Poems Selected and New* by Ed Ochester
*Rabbis of the Air* by Philip Terman
*The River Is Rising* by Patricia Jabbeh Wesley
*Let It Be a Dark Roux* by Sheryl St. Germain
*Dixmont* by Rick Campbell
*The Dark Opens* by Miriam Levine ● 2007, selected by
  Mark Doty
▲ *The Song of the Horse* by Samuel Hazo
*My Life as a Doll* by Elizabeth Kirschner
*She Heads into the Wilderness* by Anne Marie Macari
*When She Named Fire: An Anthology of Contemporary Poetry*
  *by American Women* edited by Andrea Hollander Budy
*67 Mogul Miniatures* by Raza Ali Hasan
*House Where a Woman* by Lori Wilson
*A Theory of Everything* by Mary Crockett Hill ● 2008, selected
  by Naomi Shihab Nye
*What the Heart Can Bear* by Robert Gibb
*Blood Honey* by Chana Bloch
*The White Museum* by George Bilgere
*The Gift That Arrives Broken* by Jacqueline Berger ● 2009,
  selected by Alicia Ostriker

      ● Winner of the annual Autumn House Poetry Prize
      ▲ Hardcover

## DESIGN AND PRODUCTION

Cover and text design by Kathy Boykowycz
Cover painting: "Pines in Fog," by Nancy Clark

Set in Frutiger fonts, designed in 1975 by Adrian Frutiger

Printed by BookMobile